SRA Open Court Reading

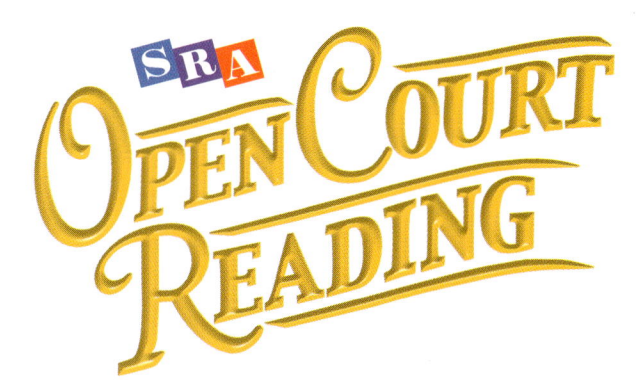

Grab a Star

SRA

A Division of The McGraw·Hill Companies

Columbus, Ohio

www.sra4kids.com

SRA/McGraw-Hill

*A Division of The **McGraw·Hill** Companies*

Copyright © 2002 by SRA/McGraw-Hill.

All rights reserved. Except as permitted under the United States Copyright Act, no part of this publication may be reproduced or distributed in any form or by any means, or stored in a database or retrieval system, without prior written permission from the publisher.

Printed in the United States of America.

Send all inquiries to:
SRA/McGraw-Hill
8787 Orion Place
Columbus, OH 43240-4027

ISBN 0-07-569474-3

3 4 5 6 7 8 9 DBH 05 04 03 02

"Mom, are stars far off?" asked Max.
"Yes, Max," said Mom.
"Stars are far, far away."

"Mom, can I grab stars for fun?" asked Max.
"Hmmm…grab stars for fun…," said Mom.

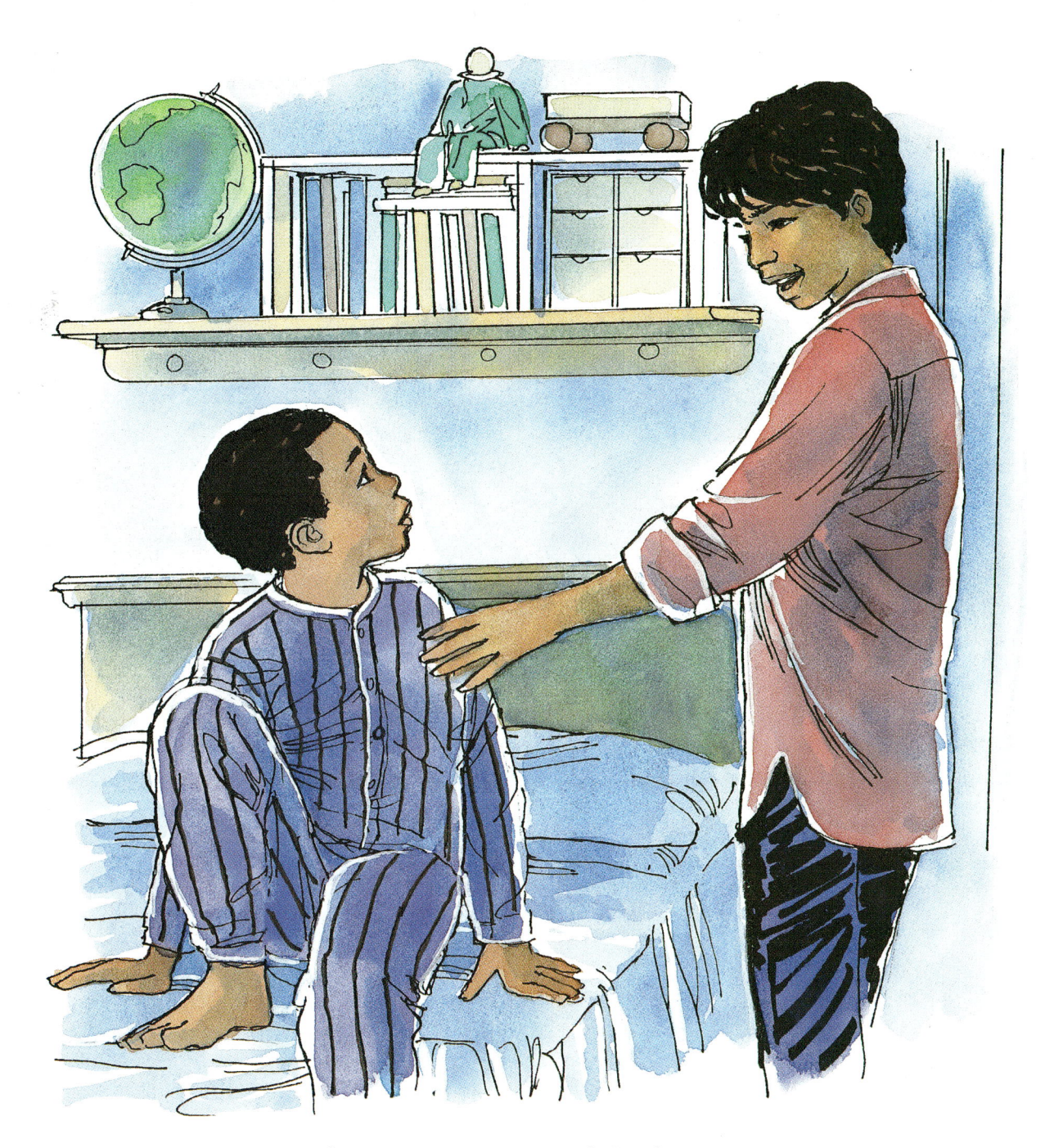

"Sit here, Max," added Mom.
"You can catch stars for fun."

Max said, "Stars are so far.
I can't have stars."

"Max," called Mom.
"This is a star you can catch!"

"I can catch stars!" said Max.
"Mom, you are smart!"